Contents

Time to eat.....................4

Tongue tastes..................6

Sweet and salty...............8

Sour and spicy..............10

Food smells....................12

Animal noses.................14

Warning smells.............16

Keeping clean...............18

Seasonal smells.............20

Notes for adults............22

Index..........................24

Time to eat

Mmmmmm!

What have you cooked?
It smells good!

4

Tasting and Smelling

Katie Dicker

First published in paperback 2011,
by Evans Brothers Limited
2A Portman Mansions
Chiltern Street
London W1U 6NR

Produced for Evans Brothers Limited by
White-Thomson Publishing Ltd

Printed by Everbest in China
July 2011, job number (CAG1678)
Printed on chlorine-free paper from sustainably managed sources.

Educational consultant: Sue Palmer MEd FRSA FEA
Project manager: Katie Dicker
Picture research: Amy Sparks
Design: Balley Design Limited
Creative director: Simon Balley
Designer/Illustrator: Michelle Tilly/Andrew Li

The activities in this book are designed to be used at the discretion of the pre-school
practitioner, teacher or parent/guardian. The publisher shall not be liable for any
accidents, losses or malpractices arising from or relating to these activities.

British Library Cataloguing in Publication Data

Dicker, Katie
   Tasting and smelling. - (My senses) (Sparklers)
   1. Smell - Pictorial works - Juvenile literature 2. Taste -
   Pictorial works - Juvenile literature
   I. Title
   612.8'6

ISBN: 978 0 2375 4449 2

Tasty!

What do YOU like to eat?

Tongue tastes

Yummy!

Your tongue senses different tastes.

Can YOU guess what food you are eating?

7

Sweet and salty

juicy!

These **strawberries** **taste** sweet.

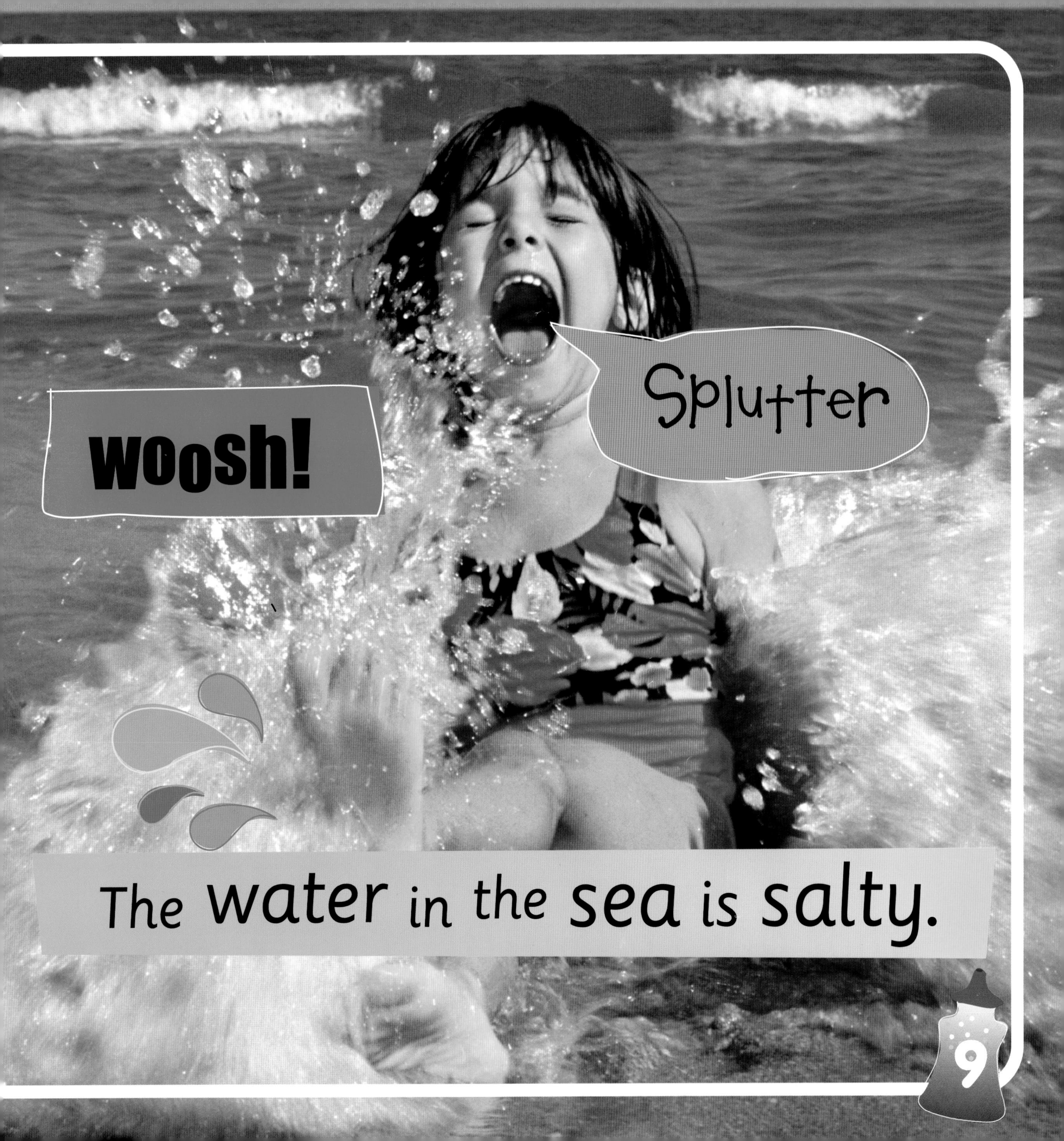

woosh!

Splutter

The **water** in the **sea** is **salty**.

9

Sour and spicy

Eeeee-oooo-ug!

What does a lemon taste like?

red hot!

Some spices taste very HOT!

Food Smells

Delicious!

Food often **tastes** the way that it **smells.**

This fish market is full of seaside smells.

Animal noses

Dogs have a very strong sense of smell.

Sniff

Sniff

Elephants can **smell** danger that is **miles** away!

15

Warning smells

Poo–eee!

Our noses tell us when food has gone bad.

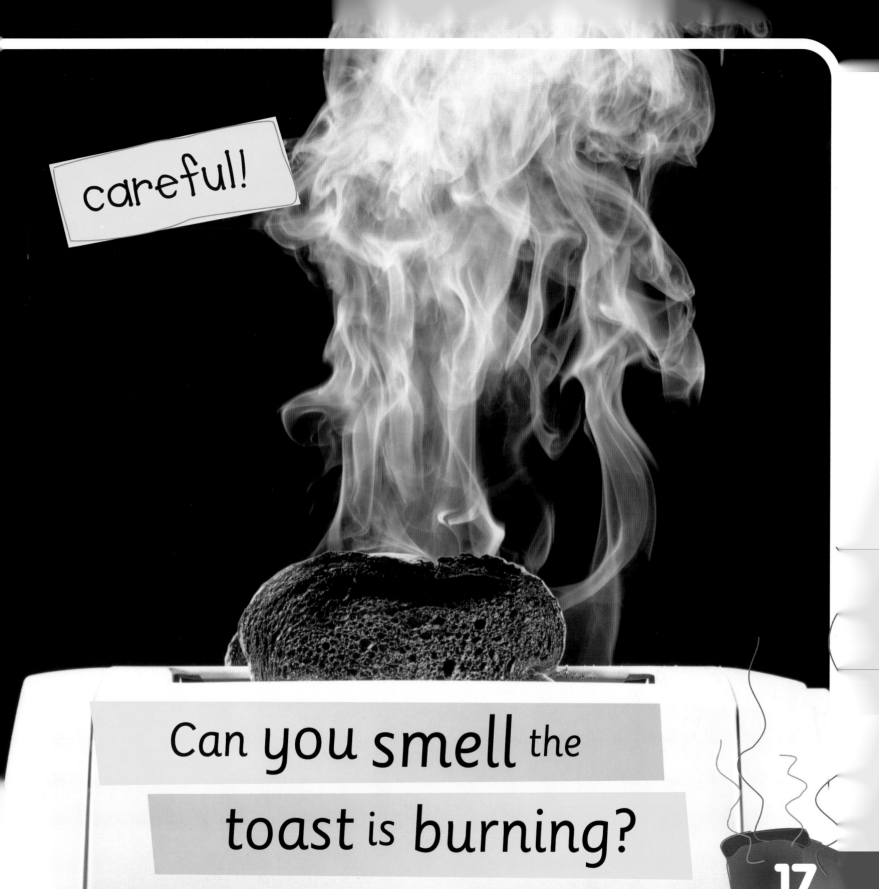

careful!

Can you smell the toast is burning?

17

Keeping clean

bubbles

When we wash,

we smell clean and fresh.

18

These autumn leaves
smell dusty.

deep breath!

Which smells remind you of spring and summer?

21

Notes for adults

Sparklers books are designed to support and extend the learning of young children. The **Food We Eat** titles won a Practical Pre-School Sliver Award, the **Body Moves** titles won a Practical Pre-School Gold Award and the **Out and About** titles won the 2009 Practical Pre-School Gold Overall Winner Award. The books' high-interest subjects link in to the Early Years Foundation Stage curriculum and beyond. Find out more about Early Years and reading with children from the National Literacy Trust (www.literacytrust.org.uk).

Themed titles

Tasting and Smelling is one of four **Senses** titles that explore the five senses of sight, touch, smell, taste and sound. The other titles are:

Seeing   **Hearing**   **Touching and Feeling**

Areas of learning

Each **Senses** title helps to support the following Foundation Stage areas of learning:

Personal, Social and Emotional Development
Communication, Language and Literacy
Mathematical Development
Knowledge and Understanding of the World
Physical Development
Creative Development

Making the most of reading time

When reading with younger children, take time to explore the pictures together. Ask children to find, identify, count or describe different objects. Point out colours and textures. Allow quiet spaces in your reading so that children can ask questions or repeat your words. Try pausing mid-sentence so that children can predict the next word. This sort of participation develops early reading skills.

Follow the words with your finger as you read. The main text is in Infant Sassoon, a clear, friendly font designed for children learning to read and write. The labels and sound effects add fun and give the opportunity to distinguish between levels of communication. Where appropriate, labels, sound effects or main text may be presented phonically. Encourage children to imitate the sounds.

As you read the book, you can also take the opportunity to talk about the book itself with appropriate vocabulary such as "page", "cover", "back", "front", "photograph", "label" and "page number".

You can also extend children's learning by using the books as a springboard for discussion and further activities. There are a few suggestions on the facing page.

Pages 4–5: Time to eat

Collect some empty pots (plastic yoghurt or cream pots are useful, with punched holes in the lid) and fill each one with a common food, such as onion, banana, vinegar, peanut butter, coffee granules, tomato ketchup, vanilla essence, peppermint and lemon. You may want to use cotton wool to soak the liquids, to avoid spillage. Ask children to identify what they can smell.

Pages 6–7: Tongue tastes

Encourage children to identify the four tastes of bitter, sour, sweet and salty. Take four glasses of water and make a different mixture in each one using a little instant coffee, lemon juice, sugar and salt. Which tastes can the children identify? Which do they like best?

Pages 8–9: Sweet and salty

Cut different pictures of food from magazines and ask children to identify whether the foods are sweet or savoury. Ask children to think about what they eat for lunch or dinner. Do they tend to eat sugary foods first or last? Do the children know any dishes that have a sweet and savoury flavour? The Mexican dish of chocolate chicken is one example.

Pages 10–11: Sour and spicy

Children may enjoy playing 'Spice' ladders. Group the children in pairs and ask them to sit facing each other with their legs outstretched, in a long line. Give each pair a 'spice' name, such as 'chilli', 'paprika' or 'cumin'. Make up a fictional story about preparing a curry – when you mention a 'spice', the appropriate pair has to run a full circuit between the pairs of legs to the end, round and back to their place. You could even introduce trick words such as 'I was feeling a bit chilly'! The winner is the team on the left/right who gets most runners back first.

Pages 12–13: Food smells

Prepare some pieces of pear, apple and orange. Ask the children to close their eyes and to hold their nose. Can they identify the different tastes without their sense of smell? Now ask them to hold an onion slice under their nose while eating the pear, apple or orange. What do they taste this time?

Pages 14–15: Animal noses

Cut photographs from magazines showing animals and different types of food. Ask children to match the animal with their favourite smell – such as dog with a bone and seagull with a fish.

Pages 16–17: Warning smells

Ask children to sit in a group and spray a little perfume on one side of the room. Ask the children to raise their hand when they can smell the perfume. Explain the way that smells, such as smoke, travel through the air. Reiterate the importance of using the senses together to act safely.

Pages 18–19: Keeping clean

Children may enjoy making their own perfume. Fill a cup with water and add some chopped flower blossom to the water – flowers with strong smells such as lilac, lavender, orange blossom or honeysuckle work best. Leave the mixture overnight and then strain with a sieve. Which perfumes would the children choose to make a fresh-smelling soap or washing powder?

Pages 20–21: Seasonal smells

Children may enjoy making a season collage. Ask children to think of the different smells of spring, summer, autumn and winter. Divide a large piece of card into four squares, and ask the children to draw the smells in each 'season' quarter. They could also use photographs cut from magazines.

Index

a

animals **14, 15**
autumn **20**

c

clothes **19**
cooking **4**

d

danger **15, 17**

e

eating **5, 7**

f

food **7, 12, 16**

l

leaves **20**
lemon **10**

n

nose **16**

s

salty **9**
sea **9, 13**
smell **4, 12, 13, 14, 15, 17, 18, 19, 20, 21**
spices **11**
spring **21**
strawberries **8**
summer **21**
sweet **8**

t

taste **6, 8, 10, 11, 12**
tongue **6**

w

washing **18, 19**

Picture acknowledgements:
Alamy: 5 (Serge Bogomyako); **Corbis:** 8 (B. Bird/zefa), 11 (John Miller/Robert Harding World Imagery), 18 (Heide Benser/zefa), 19 (Graham Bell); **Getty Images:** 4 (VEER Steve Cicero/Photonica), 7 (Image Source), 9 (Carlos Davila), 10 (Robert Daly), 12 (Johner Images), 15 (Tim Fitzharris), 17 (GK Hart/Vicky Hart); **IStockphoto:** cover tablecloth (Jon Helgason), cover sky (Judy Foldetta); **Photolibrary:** 13 (Aykan Ozener); **Shutterstock:** cover (Gelpi), 2-3 fruit (Julián Rovagnati), 6 (Julián Rovagnati), 14 (Vadim Eddy), 16 (Julie DeGuia), 20 (Jun Li), 21 (Anna Kaminska), 22-23 vegetables, 24 vegetables (Hannamariah).